STEVEN CLARK

Body Language

Understand How Non-Verbal Communication Works To Persuade And Analyze People Through Body Language

Copyright © 2021 Steven Clark

All rights reserved.

© **Copyright 2021 - All rights reserved.**

The content contained within this book may not be reproduced, duplicated or transmitted without direct written permission from the author or the publisher.

Under no circumstances will any blame or legal responsibility be held against the publisher, or author, for any damages, reparation, or monetary loss due to the information contained within this book. Either directly or indirectly.

Legal Notice:

This book is copyright protected. This book is only for personal use. You cannot amend, distribute, sell, use, quote or paraphrase any part, or the content within this book, without the consent of the author or publisher.

Disclaimer Notice:

Please note the information contained within this document is for educational and entertainment purposes only. All effort has been executed to present accurate, up to date, and reliable, complete information. No warranties of any kind are declared or implied. Readers acknowledge that the author is not engaging in the rendering of legal, financial, medical or professional advice. The content within this book has been derived from various sources. Please consult a licensed professional before attempting any techniques outlined in this book.

By reading this document, the reader agrees that under no circumstances is the author responsible for any losses, direct or indirect, which are incurred as a result of the use of information contained within this document, including, but not limited to, — errors, omissions, or inaccuracies.

Table of Content

Introduction 4
Chapter 1. How Non-Verbal Communication Works.................... 12
Chapter 2. How to Understand People Through Body Language 22
Chapter 3. Manipulation Through Body Language 31
Chapter 4. Uses of Body Language.. 37
Chapter 5. Guide to an Effective Body Language 44
Chapter 6. How to Persuade People 51
Chapter 7. How to Analyze People 58
Chapter 8. Dark Psychology Secrets 65
Chapter 9. How to Defend Ourselves of Dark Psychology 72
Conclusion.. 80

Introduction

Body language involves using our physical behavior, expressions, and manners to reveal nonverbal information about ourselves, which is usually done unconsciously. Many people are not mindful of it, but you are continually giving out body cues and wordless signals that reinforce the interaction or contradict what you are trying to say in all your interactions.

Your entire nonverbal behavior transmits a loud and strong message that continues even after you stop talking. There are instances when what someone says might differ from what their body language is communicating. Hence, in this case, it will be easy for the person you are interacting with to pass you off as a liar. If someone asked for a favor and you gave a smile after giving a no, you have ended up confusing the person. With this kind of mixed-signal, the person might be confused about what to believe. However, if the person understands the concept of body language, they would probably just walk away since the body language is unconscious and gives someone away by revealing their real intention.

The Essence of Nonverbal Communication

The cues you are unconsciously giving out from your body are pretty essential and, as said earlier, give meaning to the interaction you are in. From your body cues, the person you are with will know whether you are interested in the relationship or not, whether you are hiding information or being explicit, and whether you are paying attention.

With nonverbal communication signals that complement what you say, you can build trust, rapport, and clarity. I am pretty sure you know what happens when your words and body language cues contrast!

In reading body language signals, you have to notice the body language people are giving out. It does not stop at that, and you have to be sensitive to yours as well. In understanding nonverbal communication, pay attention to the following roles it plays:

Repetition

In other words, it enforces the message you are trying to pass. You made a marriage proposal to your girlfriend, for instance. After popping the question and she accepted, you would generally expect her to smile, jump up and be excited. However, if she said yes with a straight face, I am pretty sure you know something is not right.

Contradiction

It can also refute the message you pass across, thus giving the signal that you might be lying. You came home from a two-week journey. Your wife greeted you and said she was excited to see you, but without a hug, a smile, or any facial expression to corroborate the statement. Something was off.

Substitution

Body cues often stand in place of verbal communication. In African culture, for instance, let us assume a guest visited a family. As this person was leaving, he offered the child some money. The mother gave the child "that kind of look," and the child took it as a cue to reject the offer.

Complementing

Body language cues might add more weight to the meaning of the message you are passing across verbally. Consider a man who tells his wife, "I love you" and drives off. Another man plants a kiss on the wife's forehead and says, "I love you" while looking into her eyes. Of these two, it is clear which one meant what he was saying.

Accenting

Your nonverbal cues can also emphasize the point you are trying to make. Saying no, alongside a shaking of the head, emphasizes the weight of the negation.

Without beating around the bush any more, let us examine how you can read various clues from body parts.

Reading Various Parts of the Body

Head Movement

Head movement is one of the meekest body languages to decode. However, for someone who has no clue what this nonverbal communication signal means, hardly will they make sense of it. To explain the head movement, I have here two scenarios:

As part of the exercise to get a job, a candidate must decide why he is the best candidate for the job. During the presentation, his audience, the hiring manager, nods quickly while the candidate desperately keeps trying to sell himself. He is unaware of the hiring manager's message, which clearly shows he is wasting his time.

Consider another candidate giving the same presentation. As he goes off trying to sell himself, the hiring manager leans back with his head tilted. Oblivious to the meaning of this body language, the candidate does not try to shed light on the point that triggered the manager's body reaction. He is ignorant of the body language; hence, he keeps on blabbing.

Reading the Face

There are many expressions we can reveal with our faces. Even babies and toddlers are smart enough to decode this body language cue. That a smile reveals happiness or satisfaction or a frown shows dissatisfaction or sadness. There are times when the facial expression could give insight into what is going on with a person. A person who says they're fine with a slight frown, for instance, could be lying.

It is a universal expression that conveys a wide range of emotions, such as sadness, fear, panic, anxiety, worry, disgust, distrust, happiness, and many others. The best part is that this expression does not change or vary with people.

Many people, in a bid to hide their real intention, desperately try to control the face. However, a careful study of the face can give you a clear glimpse into the message someone is trying to pass across. There are times when someone might hide primary body language, such as raised eyebrows, smiles, frowns, etc. Be sure to look out for the subsequent:

A warm and genuine smile does light up the whole face. It indicates happiness. It is also an unmistakable symbol that the other party is enjoying your company.

On the other hand, a phony smile is a polite way of showing approval, even if they do not enjoy the conversation or interaction. For you to detect a phony smile, take a look at the side of the eyes. The lack of crinkles is all you need to pass a smile off as fake.

The Eye Window

The eyes disclose a lot regarding a person. It explains why the eyes are referred to as the window to the soul. Besides, it is an essential and natural communication process for you to note all interactions' eyes.

In communicating with people, it is customary to note eye contact, whether someone is averting your gaze or not, the rate of blinking, and their pupils' size.

The following explains some nonverbal clues from the eyes:

Eye gaze

A person interested and paying attention to a conversation will look directly into your eyes while having a conversation. However, they might break eye contact once in a while because prolonged eye contact is rather uncomfortable. A distracted and uninterested person, on the other hand, will often break eye contact and look away. This person might be awkward or is trying to hide their true feelings.

Blinking

While blinking is an entirely natural process, the frequency matters. A person uncomfortable or in distress will blink more often. On the other hand, infrequent blinking means that a person is intentionally trying to control their eye movements.

Pupil Size

Pay attention to pupil size as it is very subtle and affected by the room's light level. However, emotions also affect pupil dilation, causing small changes in the pupil's size. It explains why someone with highly dilated eyes is either aroused or interested in a person.

Hand Movements

Some cues can easily be found from the hand's position and pattern of movement. We explain this in detail:

When someone has their hands in their pockets, they could be lacking confidence, hiding information, or just being defensive.

When a person unconsciously points to another person in a group or meeting while making a speech, there might be some common ground they share.

In communicating with someone, there is the presence of an obstacle. It is in the form of an object between you, and the person translates to the person trying to block you out. In this circumstance, your goal should be to build rapport and gain such a person's trust.

A person talking with the palms facing up is likely, to be honest. Such a person is not hiding the palm since they most likely have nothing to hide.

The Mouth

The expressions and movement of the mouth are pretty vital in decoding body language as well. It is why a worried, anxious, or insecure person will likely chew their lower lip. Some forms of nonverbal communication cues from the mouth will be examined below. A person, to be polite, might cover the mouth if the other party is yawning. Be watchful, as it can be done to cover up a frown as well.

Pursed lips

When a person tightens up their lip, it could signal objection, disapproval, or distaste.

Lip biting

It is common when a person is anxious, worried, or stressed.

Covering the Mouth

It could be done to hide emotional reactions like smiles or smirks.

A Slight Change in Direction

A person's feelings can be seen through the direction of the mouth. As a result, someone happy or in a good mood might have their mouth slightly turned up. A slightly turned-down mouth, on the other hand, could signal sadness or displeasure.

The Importance of Reading People

The world is made of people. Life is better enjoyed when you have people to relate with. However, your survival in the world also depends on your ability to decide when not cooperating with some people. So, your ability to read people is essential.

There are times you are unconsciously cooperating with others. The fact that you walk gently to your place of work without causing a scene or doing anything to warrant unnecessary attention is an act of cooperation with the rest of the society on some level. You don't just awaken up one day and choose to go on a killing spree. You are connected to the Internet and the rest of the world alike. All these things require some form of human cooperation.

For this to occur, people unconsciously have to come to an appropriate form of agreement and acceptable behavior on some level. All in all, cooperating with people is pretty important, and your decision whether to cooperate or not comes down to your ability to read people.

The best salesman knows how to coax you because they are good at analyzing people. They can get you into buying what they have to offer, even if you do not need what they are offering. The better you are at reading other people's motives, the better you can deal with such a person.

Chapter 1. How Non-Verbal Communication Works

Being able to connect well is extremely important when wanting to succeed in the personal and professional world, but it isn't the words you say that scream. It is your body language that does the screaming. Your gestures, posture, eye contact, facial expressions, and tone of voice are your best communication tools. These can confuse, undermine, offend, build trust, draw others in, or put someone at ease.

There are many times where what someone says and what their body language says is different. Non-verbal communication could do five things:

- Substitute—It could be used in place of a verbal message.

- Accent—It could underline or accent your verbal message.

- Complement—It could complement or add to what you are saying verbally.

- Repeat—It could strengthen and repeat your verbal message.

- Contradict—It could go against what you are trying to say verbally to make your listener think you are lying.

Many different forms of Non-verbal communication will be looked at, and we are going to cover:

- Gestures—These have been woven into our lives. You might speak animatedly; argue with your hands, point, wave, or beckon. Gestures do change according to cultures.

- Facial expressions—You will learn that the face is expressive and shows several emotions without speaking one word. Unlike what you say and other types of body language, facial expressions are usually universal.

- Eye contact—Because sight tends to be our strongest sense for most people, it is an essential part of Non-verbal communication. The way someone looks at you could tell you whether they are attracted to you, affectionate, hostile, or interested. It might also help the conversation flow.

- Body movement and posture—Take a moment to think about how you view people based on how they hold their heads, stand, walk around, and sit. The way a person carries gives you much information.

Lower Body

The arms share much information. The hands share a lot more, but legs give us the exclamation point and tell us precisely what someone is thinking. The legs could say to you if a person is open and comfortable. They could also imply dominance or where they want to go.

Upper Body

Upper body language can show signs of defensiveness since the arms could easily be used as a shield. Upper body language could involve the chest. Let's look at some upper body language.

Leaning

If someone leans forward, it will move them closer to another person. There are two possible meanings to this. First, it will tell you that they are interested in something, which could just be what you are talking about. But this movement could also show romantic interest. Second, leaning forward could invade a person's personal space; hence, leading to a threat. It is often an aggressive display. It is done unconsciously by influential people.

The Superman

Bodybuilders, models commonly use this, and it was made famous by Superman. It could have various meanings depending on how a person uses it. Within the animal world, animals will try to make themselves look bigger when they feel threatened. If you look at a house cat when they get spooked, they will stretch their legs, and their fur stands on end. Humans also have this, even if it isn't as noticeable. It is why we get goosebumps. Because we can't make ourselves look bigger, we have to develop arm gestures like putting our hands on our waist. It shows us that a person is getting ready to act assertively.

The Chest in Profile

If a person stands sideways or at a 45-degree angle, they are trying to accentuate their chest. They might also thrust out their chest, more on this in a minute. Women do this posture to show off their breasts, and men will show off their profile.

Outward Thrust Chest

If someone pushes their chest out, they try to draw attention to this part of their body. It could also be used as a dreamy display. Women understand that men have been programmed to be aroused by breasts. If you see a woman pushing her chest out, she might be inviting intimate relations. Men will thrust out their chests to show off their chest and possibly trying to hide their gut. The difference is that men will do this to women and other men.

Hands

Human hands have 27 bones, and they are a very expressive part of the body. It gives us much capability to handle our environment.

Reading palms isn't about just looking at the lines on the hands. After a person's face, the hands are the best source for body language. Hand gestures are different across cultures, and one hand gesture might be innocent in one country but very offensive in another.

Hand signals may be small, but they show what our subconscious is thinking. A gesture might be exaggerated and done using both hands to illustrate a point

Face

People's facial expressions could help us figure out if we trust or believe what they are saying. The most trustworthy expression will have a slight smile and a raised eyebrow. This expression will sow friendliness and confidence.

We make judgments about how intelligent somebody is by their facial expressions. People who have narrow faces with a prominent nose were thought to be extremely intelligent. People who smile and have joyous expressions could be thought of as being smart rather than someone who looks angry.

Mouth

Mouth movements and expressions are needed when trying to read body language. Chewing on their lower lip might indicate a person who is feeling fearful, insecure, or worrying.

If they cover their mouth, this might show that they are trying to be polite if they are yawning or coughing. It might be an effort to cover up disapproval. Smiling is the best signal, but smiles can be interpreted in many ways. Smiles can be genuine, or they might be used to show cynicism, sarcasm, or false happiness.

Negative Emotions

The silent signals that you show might harm your business without you even knowing it. We have over 250,000 facial signals and 700,000 body signals. Having poor body language could damage your relationships by sending other signs that you can't be trusted. They might turn off, alienate, or offend other people.

You have to keep your body language in check, and this takes much effort. Most of the time, you may not know that you are doing it, and you might be hurting your business and yourself.

Here are some emotions and how to spot them:

Fear, Anxiety, or Nervousness

Fear could happen when our basic needs get threatened. There are many different levels of fear. Suppose might be mild anxiety or full-blown blind terror. The various bodily changes that get created by fear can make this one easy to spot.

- Voice trembling.

- Errors in speech.

- Pulse rate extremely high.
- Vocal tone variations.
- Sweating.
- Lips trembling.
- Muscle tensions like their legs wrapped around something, clenched hands or arms, elbows are drawn in, jerky movements.
- Damp eyes.
- Holding their breath or gasping for breath.
- Not looking at one another.
- Fidgeting.
- Dry mouth indicated by licking their lips, rubbing their throat, or drinking water.
- Defensive body language.
- Face is pale.
- Fight or flight body language.
- Breaking out in a cold sweat.
- Any symptoms of stress.

Sadness

- Lips trembling.

- The flat tone of voice.
- Body drooping.
- Tears.

Anger

- Clenched fists.
- Invading body space.
- Leaning forward.
- Baring their teeth or snaring.
- Using aggressive body language.
- Neck or face is red and flushed.
- Displaying power body language.

Embarrassment

- Not making eye contact.
- Looking down and away.
- Neck or face is red and flushed.
- Changing the subject or trying to hide their embarrassment.
- Grimacing.
- Fake smiles.

Positive Emotions

When you have positive body language, it means that you are engaging, approachable, and open. It isn't saying that you need to use this kind of body language all the time or that it is the best signs that will show a person is friendly. It's just a good beginning point for reading positivity in others as well as yourself.

Non-verbal Signals Used Universally

Non-verbal communication is different for everybody and in different cultures. A person's cultural background will define their non-verbal communication since some communication types, like signs and signals, need to be learned.

Since there are different meanings in non-verbal communication, there could be miscommunication when people from different cultures try to communicate. People might offend others without really meaning to due to cultural differences. Facial expressions are very similar around the world.

Seven micro expressions are universal, and we will go more in-depth about these, but they are hate/contempt, anger, disgust, surprise, fear, happiness, and sadness. It might be different in the extent of how people show these feelings since, in specific cultures, people might readily show them where others won't.

Nods might also have different meanings, and this can cause problems, too. In some cultures, their people might not say "yes," but people from different cultures will interpret as "no." If you nod in Japan, they will solve it as you are listening to them.

Here are other non-verbal communications and how they differ in various cultures:

Eye Contact

Many Western cultures consider eye contact as a good gesture. It shows confidence, attentiveness, and honesty. Cultures such as Hispanic, Asian, Native American, and Middle Eastern don't think eye contact is a good gesture. They believe it is rude and offensive.

Unlike Western cultures that think it's respectful, others don't think this way. In Eastern countries, women absolutely can't make eye contact with men since it shows the power or sexual interest. Many cultures accept gazes as only showing an expression, but staring is thought of as rude in most.

Gestures

You need to be careful doing a "thumbs up" because it is very different in many cultures. Some view it as meaning "okay," but in Latin America, it is vulgar. Japan views it as meaning money.

Snapping your finger may be acceptable in some cultures, but it is disrespectful and offensive in others. In some Middle Eastern countries, showing your feet can be offensive. Pointing your finger is an insult in some cultures. People in Polynesia will stick their tongue out when they greet someone, but other cultures see it as a sign of mockery.

Touch

Touch is thought of as rude in most cultures. Some cultures look at shaking hands to be acceptable. Kissing and hugs, along with other touches, are looked at differently in different cultures. Asians are too conservative with these types of communications.

Patting someone's head or shoulder has different meanings in different cultures. Patting a child's head in Asia is extremely bad since their head is the sacred part of their body. Middle Eastern countries think people of opposite genders touching to be horrible character traits.

How and where a person gets touched could change the meaning of that touch. You need to be careful if you travel to various places.

Appearance

It is an acceptable form of non-verbal communication. Their appearance has always judged people. Differences in clothing and racial differences could tell a lot about anyone.

Making yourself look good is an important personality trait in many cultures. What is thought to be a good appearance will vary from country to country. How modest you get is measured by your appearance.

Chapter 2. How to Understand People Through Body Language

The Capital Importance of Body Language

Our bodies cannot show anything but what is in us. Our emotions use the sounding board. Therefore, we understand that our body's non-verbal part of communication always reflects our mental state, whatever the situation. Indeed, where does it come from, if not our psyche?

Body language is subject to physical law: energy does not vanish; it transforms. As electricity becomes light, heat, or movement, our psyche becomes body language.

Beware, the same gesture may have different meanings. For example, a person with arms crossed, a gesture generally interpreted as a negative signal. Indeed, arms crossed the pass to outsource refusal, withdrawal, skepticism, antipathy, etc. Sometimes this interpretation is accurate, but not always. What about a man struck, waiting for the bus? Is it expressly rejected? If so, to whom? Facing the bus? To other people like him at the bus stop? What if nobody exists? In this situation, arms crossed indicate nothing but being able to do nothing but wait. No reason to move, our man folds his arms.

To correctly decipher body language, you must first consider the action context. Also, as with verbal language, an "expression" that does not fit into a situation will have a high potential for misunderstanding.

Incorrect posture can reveal insecurity, fear, distrust, etc. On the other hand, the right posture gives the impression of strength, power, and confidence.

Understand more about using body signals to convey the desired impression.

Negative Body Language

Often, during a conversation, you can pass negative body language without realizing it.

Facial expressions and gestures end up showing several details.

Some negative postures that you should avoid in your client meetings:

- Hands-on-hips or pockets;
- Knees pointing to the exit door;
- Legs wide open;
- Crossed arms.

These attitudes are perceived, even if unconsciously, by the other person and can ruin a sale's progress.

Know other signs you should avoid avoiding transmitting the wrong body language.

Hand to Mouth

Experts analyze that when a person is not telling the truth, they usually cover their mouths.

Disparities of this posture habit are:

- Rub your lips;
- Dash the chin;
- Put stuff in front of the mouth.

Compressed Lips

Another negative body language is to compress your lips.

This act shows that the person is trying to avoid saying what he thinks.

That is, hiding your lips reveals that you don't want to answer any questions.

Defocused Look

Body language says a lot by looking.

A look without focus, or looking up and to the right, indicates confusion.

It is because, when looking away, the person is looking for a mental image.

Therefore, he shows a lack of clarity in his speech, as well as insecurity.

Forehead Contracted

In conversation, if the other person wrinkles his forehead, that's not a good sign.

These horizontal lines show a certain level of tension, doubt, or nervousness, which is a bad sign of body language.

Restricted Hand and Arm Movements

Keeping your hands behind your back or clinging to your body conveys the message of little confidence.

Another gesture to be avoided is to put your hands back or feet crossed behind the chair.

These are signs of discomfort.

Reading Body Language

Reading body language may help to assess the feeling behind or instead of the words spoken. The adult can quickly and instinctively understand that a child is frightened by thunder when they see the child screaming and covering their ears. However, there are misconceptions about body language, causing miscommunication unless the whole-body language is read.

The eyes have long been named the windows to the soul, and it may be this concept that created the greatest myth in reading bodies. It is widely assumed that if a person avoids eye contact or does not hold it, that person does not say the facts. It is a mistaken assumption though popularly known. Pathological liars may maintain sustained contact with the eyes because they realize most people assume that looking away from the eyes shows an untruth. People who say the truth do not keep eye contact because they clearly state evidence and feel no need to convince anyone of this.

When a person is depressed or uncomfortable, and avoidance of eye contact occurs. For example, a child being chastised by a parent would always look down on the ground instead of him looking in the parent's eyes. Painfully shy or nervous people, too, are having a tough time meeting another person's eyes in conversation. Someone with little actual knowledge of reading body language would find the people lying by the standard error in each of these instances. Instead, the child shows authority, the adult, contrite, and the shy person shows typical distress or uncomforted sign.

In addition to the eye movement, the overall body language used needs to be looked at. Fidgeting, drumming fingers, or playing with hair matched to a lack of eye contact shows that a person is dissatisfied with the situation or discussion topic. Still, eyes fixed on a distant point by a person with arms crossed, attentive to the conversation, shows, instead, serious attention and intense thinking on the topic of discussion.

The precise interpretation of body language may provide an insight into another person's thoughts, feelings, and emotions. However, to read correctly, it is essential to remember to look at the entire body's movements, or words, rather than treating part of the body as separate from the other parts.

Keys to Reading Body Language

Body language is the type of communication a person uses to respond to circumstances, including facial expressions. More than 54% of the way we communicate with each other consists of body language, 39% consists of how the voice is used, and just 7% consists of the words spoken. Developing one's ability to interpret and understand gestures and signs of body language would greatly benefit because it will help better understand and interact with other human beings.

Body language involves body expressions, gestures, eye contact, muscle tension, skin coloring, breathing rate, etc. Of course, you should remember that body language is different from people to people and various nationalities and cultures. Consequently, it is at all times good to check what is seen in a person. It can be achieved by answering similar questions and endeavoring to better-known individuals.

There is also a lot of myths about interpreting body language. Most deceptive books and internet guides don't teach people the right thing. There's the truth you need to learn about this, while popular reasoning can trick you into believing a person's ability to read body language is the real secret to finding lies. Some important body language secrets are:

Posture

In most situations, if you take the correct pose, you should build the right impression on people. Leaning a little towards a person can create an image of friendliness. It could also be that you have an interest in others. At the same time, seeing a level head establishes a sense of self-assurance and trust.

Legs

When a person is anxious, the legs are always moving around. It happens when the person tells lies and is bored too. It is safer to keep those legs crossed or even to give the opposite impression, to appear confident and polite to others.

Eye contact

If you keep healthy eye contact, you show concern and respect for others. And you still need to find a balance. When you hold too much eye contact, the other person would feel self-conscious. Sometimes, if you don't have enough eye contact, you can make the other person believe you're not involved in what's being addressed.

Arms

If you have primary arms crossed, you can make yourself look nervous or defensive. On the other hand, if you hold open arms, you will make yourself comfortable and embrace others.

Distance

If you hold a person close, you can make yourself look pushy or put yourself in his face. At the same time, keep a distance away may mean that you don't care about what's being addressed or don't care about it at all.

You can study a lot regarding other people through body language. Many people show all sorts of thoughts in the way they push the body. Here are examples of how to discover other people's opinions:

Confidence

A comfortable person will always stand tall, holding eye contact sold while smiling at you simultaneously. The person can go even further with the hands when making gestures.

Tips for Reading Body Language

Eye movement, gestures, posture, and facial expressions are characteristics of human body language. American human behavior expert Eric Barker explains that it is best to look at "unconscious behaviors that are not easily controlled and may contain a message." Can anyone decipher this language? Barker reveals eight tips.

Use Common Sense

For the expert, analyzing the context is essential. Crossing your arms can mean adopting a defensive posture or even trying to deceive you. However, if it is cold or if the person concerned is sitting in an armless chair, the meaning can be different (much more straightforward and harmless).

Observe the Mime

Imitating a gesture or verbal expression may mean that the person is in tune with you. The act of agreeing with someone or something is difficult to fake, so the expert believes that the best thing is to think in these cases.

Nerve Energy

The other's level of activity can reveal your interest and enthusiasm for what you are saying. Research from the University of Manchester in England states that women shake their feet when they are interested in a man. Men, on the other hand, are tending to do so when they are nervous.

Consistency

Someone who reveals a fluid and consistent speech, emphasizing certain words, demonstrates control and concentration. Showing determination as they speak, these people are difficult to influence (and seduce).

Don't Care About Individual Signs

It is not possible to distinguish what a person means by body language through a single action. It is best to look at the actions as a whole, as two or three signals can help identify what goes in the other person's head.

Create A Reference

Uneasiness and the habit of always talking do not necessarily reveal any problem. However, something may be wrong when these people suddenly become calm.

Consider Your Previous Considerations

A judgment about another person will be affected if you have an initial impression, whether positive or negative. The inclination is to give the benefit of the doubt to someone you think is similar to you.

The Most Significant Thing Is to Focus on The Whole Context

Eric Barker argues that the ability to understand body language will increase when "understanding that body language is part of a larger context. Then you will begin to pay attention to other facets of interaction: voice, appearance, clothing, etc."

Chapter 3. Manipulation Through Body Language

After leaving the University heading to the golden paved streets of London, a man saw a woman who was also a model for the entire newspaper—at this point in his life. He hadn't met anyone attractive in the real world. Every day he walked and tried to be friendly, even cool, and afterward, he knew that he had just made himself a fool!

Why did trump react to her in that way? How was it that she was so successful? Have you ever addressed people with a lack of trust? And what about those other people in his class-his friend knew almost nothing about them as adults, he had never really been told, but he wasn't shocked by their performance.

They all had a certain aura about them that all these people could have a hypnotic effect on the people around them without opening their mouths. He wants to talk about this hypnotic body language today because it can help you achieve more and perfection without really having to do so much other than subtly alter your non-verbal communication.

3 Non-verbal keys for Hypnotic communication:

True Smile and Real Laughter

He can remember when his parents invited friends for supper when he was a child when his mother always told him to make sure that he was smiling and to show his teeth when the guests were arriving (I was never cheeky enough to grow, although the man was tempted). His mother knew that smiles produced positive reactions from people on an intuitive level.

This man speaks here of a real, genuine smile—a smile from the center of your body, which reflects joy. A natural smile makes the eyes and face wrinkle; insincere people smile with their mouths alone. Genuine smiles are often from the subconscious mind; individuals can sense, see, and feel real. A genuine smile implies you smile all over your face-your muscles move, your cheeks rise, your eyes shrink, and your eyebrows slightly go down.

Smile more, then. However, smile happily, fun, and joyfully. Smile in the future.

The explanation of why a photographer uses 'cheese' is because it's a term that helps you relax your face muscles. It often gives a crooked smile. How many pictures did you see that the smiles are cheese-powered and not authentic?

Professor Ruth Campbell, University College London, says that in the brain there is a "mirror neuron" which triggers the neurology responsible for the acknowledgment of face expressions and causes an immediate, unconscious mirroring response. The world smiles at you once you smile. In other words, know it or not, very often the facial expressions we see are unintentionally expressed.

So, if you smile more often than not-people around you smile more sincerely-it means, they feel better about you. You build for yourself and others around you a better immediate environment. How would you feel if you walk down the street and seeing someone with such an unhappy or cross face? Science has exposed that the more you smile, the more positive reactions people give you.

Would you smile more if you watch a funny movie with friends? Robert Provine found that Laughter in people in social situations was more than 30 times more likely than alone. He discovered that Laughter has less to do with jokes and funny storytelling and more to do with relationship building. Laughter creates a connection.

If you smile (a real smile) at another man, they almost always return the smile with a genuine smile that gives both of you and you genuinely positive feelings because of cause and effect. It creates a cycle of comfort: you smile, and you feel the perfect smile, and feel good, etc.

Studies show that most meetings run smoother, last longer, have better results, and improve relationships dramatically if you make a point of regularly smiling and laughing until it becomes a custom. He guesses you already knew all this-yet you smile a lot. Does recent research show that we smile 400% more-how as a kid often? Do you smile at the world today?

Confidence

The person was missing when he was younger, embarrassingly answering the receptionist.

I remember watching a documentary about a schoolgirl murdered in Great Britain. The girl's parents gave a press conference calling for help in the apprehension of the killer. It was the fall of the murderers. The way the father behaved at this press conference prompted the police to suspect him and to show him that he killed his daughter at last.

Many criminals are caught not because they have clues but because they are responsible, conscious of themselves, and lack trust. These feelings are sufficiently communicated to create suspicions.

When we are emotionally congruent and trustworthy, our body language is positive and expresses it to the world.

Psychologists advise us that by modifying our physical actions, we can alter our attitudes. Thus, adopting the physiology of trust can help you appear and become more trustworthy. When you are confident and hold your body that way more often, cause and effect mean having your body feel secure.

I recall reading a book a little while ago, and it taught you three great ways to build confidence with your body alone: first, he suggested that you be a' front seater.' Wherever you go to movies, classrooms, meetings, and presentations, the back lines appear to fill up fastest, aren't they? Many people go back so that they aren't too visible. It often shows a lack of confidence in him. Start sitting up today, relaxed with other people's eyes, and build confidence.

Furthermore, making direct contact with the eyes tells you a lot about confidence. If someone avoids contact with the look, we might start wondering what's wrong with them or what they must hide. Lack of eye contact may indicate that you feel weak or that you are, in some way, afraid. Conquer this and let the person in the eye look—you don't have to stare hard! Just look in your eyes to tell them that you believe you are honest, open, confident, and comfortable.

Suppose you seem confident and think of yourself. In that case, the other person tends unconsciously to agree that there is something worth knowing about you-why should anybody else be if you aren't confident or feel good about yourself? It is implicitly conveyed beyond conscious minds, often with these sages' good feelings. David Schwartz gave the other great tip to walk 25% faster. This man knows that his father always told him to slow down when he was taken to football to see his beloved

Nottingham Forest as a boy because he was enthused and enthusiastic about their destination.

Psychologists link Slovenian stances and slowness to disagreeable attitudes towards oneself, work, and the people around us. But psychologists also tell us that by changing your posture and movement speed, you can change your attitudes. Body action is the result of mental action-and vice versa-as this man already said; cause and effect! The person with low morality is shuffling with little confidence and stumbles through life. Likewise, ordinary people are on average. You can see it, and you can hear it.

Confident people travel purposefully, they have to go somewhere important, and they will succeed when they get there. Open your chest, throw your shoulders back, lift your head, be proud of yourself, move a little faster, feel that your trust will grow. It doesn't have to be dramatic; just keep your body safe.

The Right-Hand Side of the Brain

Most people are right-handed, and as such, their thoughts and lives are processed on the right-hand side of their brain, and motor reactions and functional brain use reside on their brain's left-hand side.

Evolutionary psychologists debate it; most of them think we all have six raw emotions. All else is derived from these. Those six emotions are central: happiness. Surprise. Disgust. Fear. Rage. Anger. Sadness.

It's worth noting here that only two of them are good. If we are real, only one is guaranteed to be great to ourselves, isn't that? Following April's foolish day, he is reminded how much he enjoys' his surprise!

The vast majority of our thoughts in our minds are somehow negative. It is accurate, and bad things tend to stand out much more than our minds' good things.

So, if you respond to anybody's right brain, you may unconsciously associate yourself in the right mind with all those emotions. You don't want to do it.

If you first meet someone to use this knowledge in life instead, put yourself, so they have to look slightly right to look at you. See your right eye when you shake your hands. He believes that this picture is so much on his website's right-hand side. That in his rooms, the man places his chair so that his customers need to look correct when we communicate.

There are three powerful things to remember when improving your success and performance without opening your mouth.

Note that if you smile and smile with enthusiasm, if you behave with faith and connect with the right brain pieces, you start resonating far more gradually with the whole world.

Chapter 4. Uses of Body Language

Body language and self-esteem go hand in hand. It allows for a beautiful mechanism to observe and monitor how people behave and feel. Awareness of our body language is essential for becoming effective and persuasive communicators. Hence, there are several applications for using, reading, and changing body language.

Therapeutic Applications

Body language plays a significant role in counseling, NLP, and hypnotherapy. For psychologists, body language allows them to read their clients' emotional state and gives them a way to build rapport. Observing the client's body language can help the psychologist read how the client responds to a specific discussion or questioning line.

Body language speaks when we can't. Health care professionals have known this for some time. Many studies have been conducted in it and psychology academic studies for professionals, including modalities on body language.

Common issues which can be examined and treated through the use of body language include:

Bipolarity

Individuals with this condition suffer a chemical imbalance that leads to severe depression and the inability to make decisions.

They often have low self-esteem that accompanies this disorder, and it is incredibly challenging to understand effectively or treat correctly. The person with bipolarity can be taught to manage their daily situations. Considering the link between body language and emotion, they can also enjoy relief by being trained to use positive body language. It is a means for them to use their body language to persuade their emotions to stabilize and improve. For their families, body language reading is also an effective way to monitor their loved one's state and intervene before incidents happen. Depression can often go unnoticed, and people will rarely speak out about it. They are not likely to say: "I'm feeling depressed."

Low Self-Esteem

Many of us have suffered the disturbing effects of low self-esteem in one way or another. The first victim is our ability to progress in life. A positive belief in yourself is needed to convince the rest of the world to believe in you. People can be trained in positive body language such as open positions, eye contact, and lifting the head. It's a case of falsifying it until you feel it. With enough repetitive use of persuasive body language, you can even convince yourself that you are stronger than you believe.

Trauma

Survivors of trauma suffer from a loss of power, feelings of inadequacy, and loss of confidence. They also have the burden of guilt, where they hold themselves responsible for what happened to them. Whether the trauma is due to a violent act, these individuals' emotional state is reflected in their body language. Body language may have been positive and inviting before the incident. The person may display negative body languages, such as crossed arms, slumping, excessive facial touching, and nervous ticks such as repetitive movement. With effective counseling, their progress to recovery can be tracked through counseling and monitoring their body language.

Abuse

Abuse can be physical, emotional, and sexual, but whichever of these it is, there is bound to be an overwhelming sense of a loss of power. The victim may need to be convinced that they can regain their strength and that it is okay to trust people. Body language is extremely efficient in this regard. Helping these survivors of abuse establish strong body language will increase their sense of their strength. Suffering abuse is also linked to a loss of trust in people and the world around them.

By helping the abuse victim understand others' body language, they can be aided in evaluating the world and those around them regarding what they see, not what they fear. It is already great empowerment to the abuse victim, as they can become a participant in life again and feel like they can make informed decisions.

Self-Development

Being an effective communicator is one of life's excellent skills that will open doors and lead to the self's emboldening. Self-development programs often include body language modalities where the participants are trained in positive body language and assertiveness.

Group Dynamics

People can be classed into two groups: introverts and extroverts. Introverts, as we know, are those people who tend to thrive in one-on-one communications and prefer to spend more time alone, while extroverts are the life of the party and go through life with a the-more-the-merrier attitude. Introverts often suffer a form of depression based on social settings. They do not do well in groups. As a result, their communication within a group dynamic tends to fizzle. Yet, communication is a learned skill. As we learn the words, sentence structures, and grammar of a new language, we can also learn how body language works.

Depression

People suffering from depression tend to convince themselves that they are not worthy, that they are to blame for some usually imaginary flaw, and that everyone around them judges them.

People with depression sometimes think that everyone else has it right, while they alone are suffering. In creating awareness of body language, they can see the world in a more realistic sense and realize that people everywhere go through trying times and are not alone.

By learning to focus on using positive body language, they can also begin to manage their condition, encouraging well-being.

OCD

This condition is known for the repetitive behavior that someone engages in to make themselves feel in control of their lives. At the root of this tragic condition lies the fear of losing power and a profound distrust in themselves and others. In extreme cases, this can even encompass excessive washing of hands to remove imaginary germs and avoid people because people have germs.

People with OCD tend to have a very negative view of the world, and their only safety comes from their repetitive behaviors. Using body language, they can be trained to notice positive feelings in others and incorporate them into themselves. As they learn to project a positive self-image, they will feel their stress levels diminish, which will lead to a reduction of their anxiety-driven obsessions. When they feel more balanced, they will begin to develop trust in themselves and those around them.

Destructive Body Imagery (Bulimia and Obesity)

Low body image is a tragic and very destructive condition to suffer from. It goes with low self-esteem, lack of trust, feelings of abandonment, and severe depression. Bulimia leads the sufferer to obsessively lose weight, while obesity is a condition where the sufferer wants to fill themselves due to their emotional disabilities.

Both these conditions are associated with a loss of reality. These people begin to see the world not as it is, but as they believe it to be, and their world view is almost always negative. They eat or refuse to eat, to hide from the world and themselves.

Body language is a way to find a connection back to the real world. In reading the body language being projected by those around us, we can see that many individuals are just like us. We are not alone. Using positive body language is a therapeutic way to recover a sense of self that is realistic and beneficial.

The Biological Feedback Mechanism of Body Language

Due to our loss of trust in other humans, we often turn to animals for comfort and assurance. We read into what people do, what they say, how they say it, and how they react. A salesperson will do this on a second-by-second basis to monitor the client's body language and adjust their body language to match. Techniques such as mirroring, open position, advancing or retreating, and touching can be used to have an effect on the other person and monitor how persuasive we are on them. If they have begun to trust us enough, they will start to do something we want; in which case, we will trust them since they've done something for us. This endless, nonverbal loop is known as a biological feedback mechanism.

Training and Exercises

Some numerous academies and colleges strive to train people in body language detection and application. They mention facts and case-studies, what to do and what not to do; however, not many of them detail precisely how to improve your body language in a step-by-step way. When considering the activities and desired results, we suggest the following steps be followed:

Observe

Look at the world around you. Notice the people in it and how they interact with each other. Identify people in similar situations to those that challenge you. It could be someone applying for a promotion at work, asking a girl on a date, and even haggling for a discount. Each situation will use the same skills but in different ways. It all boils down to body language.

Practice

It will require some bravery, which is perhaps why people do crazy things in foreign lands where no one knows them. Find some friends, set up a hidden camera if you have to, or undergo obedience training with your dog. The goal is to place yourself in a situation where you can practice some of the skills and how they can be used.

If you feel overwhelmed, you can practice at home with a mirror. You might even find some online help with an online counselor who can perhaps observe you over Skype.

Evaluate

Look at the recording you made of yourself, or talk to friends who are helping you. Don't look at your awkwardness; instead, focus on each body language technique, how you applied it, and what the response to it was.

You may even give yourself a score or write down what you need to focus on. Recall rejoicing the successes, no matter how small. Then it's time to repeat step two, practice.

It may seem like an incredibly arduous task to learn body language, but it certainly is worth it. These skills of using space, posture, facial expressions, eye contact, gesture, and touch are vital to leading a fulfilling life that has less conflict and misunderstanding in it.

Chapter 5. Guide to an Effective Body Language

Research has shown that, when you are aware of your own body's happenings, you can manipulate it by training yourself to have control and even mold it to have effective communication. Further research recommends that you take some breathing exercises before going into a meeting or presentation. It will help you calm and have the ability to take note of your posture and gestures while on presentation. As you have noted by now, mirroring is a good technique. Always try to be keen on what the next person is doing non-verbally and copy that. It will help you turn out to be more effective in your communication with them. They will understand you better because this tunes your mind to communicate more truthfully at a place of relaxation.

However, you should be careful while shaping your body language. It is to ensure that the body language that you portray matches with what you are trying to present. A mismatch may bring confusion and may not be relevant at the moment. The person you are in conversation with my mistake you for meaning something else contrary to what you intended. The secret to having control of your body language is taking your time to learn it and being aware of your non-verbal cues as you apply what you know.

The Body Language That Will Help You Take Charge of Your Space

Effective management involves individuals being able to encourage and have a positive influence. In planning for a necessary appointment, maybe with your employees, management team, or partners, you focus on what to say, memorizing critical points, and rehearsing your presentation to make you feel believable and persuasive. It is something you should be conscious of, of course.

Here is what you should know if you want to control your position, at work, in presentation, or as a leader.

Seven Seconds is What You Have to Make an Impression

First impressions are essential in market relationships. When somebody psychologically marks you as trustworthy, or skeptical, strong, or submissive, you will be seen through such a filter in any other dealings that you do or say. Your partners will look for the finest in you if they like you. They will suspect all of your deeds if they distrust you. While you can't stop people from having quick decisions, as a defense mechanism, the human mind is programmed in this way. You can learn how to make these choices useful to you. In much less than seven seconds, the initial perceptions are developed and strongly influenced by body language. Studies have found that nonverbal signals have more than four times the effect on the first impression you create than you speak. It is what you should know regarding making positive and lasting first impressions. Bear in mind several suggestions here:

- Start by changing your attitude. People immediately pick up your mood. Have you noticed that you immediately get turned off after finding a customer service representative with a negative attitude? You feel like leaving or request to be served by a different person. That will happen to you, too, if you have a bad mood, which is highly noticeable. Think of the situation and make a deliberate decision about the mindset you want to represent before you meet a client, or join the meeting room for a company meeting, or step on the scene to make an analysis.

- Smile. Smiling is a good sign that leaders are under using. A smile is a message, a gesture of recognition, and acceptance. "I'm friendly and accessible," it says. Having a smile on your face will change the mood of your audience. If they had another perception of you, a smile can change that and make them relax.

- Make contact with your eyes Looking at somebody's eyes conveys vitality and expresses interest and transparency. An excellent way to help you make eye contact is to practice observing the eye color of everybody you encounter to enhance your eye contact. Overcome being shy and practice this excellent body language.

- Lean in gently the body language that has you leaning forward, expresses that you are actively participating and interested in the discussion. But be careful about the space of the other individual. It means staying about two feet away in most professional situations.

- Shaking hands. This will be the best way to develop a relationship. It's the most successful as well. Research indicates that maintaining the very same degree of partnership you can get with a simple handshake takes a minimum of three hours of intense communication. You should ensure that you have palm-to-palm touch and also that your hold is firm but not bone-crushing.

- Look at your position. Studies have found that uniqueness of posture, presenting yourself in a way that exposes your openness and takes up space, generates a sense of control that creates changes in behavior in a subject independent of its specific rank or function in an organization. In fact, in three studies, it was repeatedly found that body position was more important than the hierarchical structure in making a person think, act, and be viewed more strongly.

Building your credibility is dependent on how you align your non-verbal communication

Trust is developed by a perfect agreement between what is being said and the accompanying expressions. If your actions do not entirely adhere to your spoken statement, people may consciously or unconsciously interpret dishonesty, confusion, or internal turmoil.

By the use of an electroencephalograph (EEG) device to calculate "event-related potentials"–brain waves that shape peaks and valleys to examine gesture effects prove that one of these valleys happens when movements that dispute what is spoken are shown to subjects. It is the same dip in the brainwave that occurs when people listen to a language that does not make sense. In a somewhat reasonable way, they simply do not make sense if leaders say one thing and their behaviors point to something else. Each time your facial expressions do not suit your words. For instance, losing eye contact or looking all over the room when trying to express sincerity, swaying back on the heels while thinking about the company's bright future, or locking arms around the chest when announcing transparency. All this causes the verbal message to disappear.

What Your Hands Mean When You Use Them

Have you at any point seen that when individuals are energetic about what they're stating, their signals naturally turned out to be increasingly energized? Their hands and arms continuously move, accentuating focus, and passing on eagerness.

You might not have known about this association before. However, you intuitively felt it. Research shows that an audience will, in general, view individuals who utilize a more prominent assortment of hand motions in a progressively ideal light. Studies likewise find that individuals who convey through dynamic motioning will, in general, be assessed as warm, pleasant, and vivacious. In contrast, the individuals who stay still or whose motions appear to be mechanical or "wooden" are viewed as legitimate, cold, and systematic.

That is one motivation behind why signals are so essential to a pioneer's viability and why getting them directly in an introduction associates so effectively with a group of people. You may have seen senior administrators commit little avoidable errors. When pioneers don't utilize motions accurately on the off chance, they let their hands hang flaccidly to the side or fasten their hands before their bodies in the exemplary "fig leaf" position. It recommends they have no passionate interest in the issues or are not persuaded about the fact of the matter they're attempting to make.

To utilize signals adequately, pioneers should know how those developments will be seen in all probability. Here are four basic hand motions and the messages behind them:

- Concealed hands—Shrouded hands to make you look less reliable. It is one of the nonverbal signs that is profoundly imbued in our subliminal. Our precursors settled on endurance choices dependent on bits of visual data they grabbed from each other. In ancient times, when somebody drew nearer with hands out of view, it was a sign of potential peril. Albeit today the risk of shrouded hands is more representative than genuine, our instilled mental inconvenience remains.

- Blame game—I've frequently observed officials utilize this signal in gatherings, arrangements, or meetings for accentuation or to show strength. The issue is that forceful blame dispensing can recommend that the pioneer lose control of the circumstance, and the signal bears a resemblance to parental reprimanding or play area harassing.

- Eager gestures—There is an intriguing condition of the hand and arm development with vitality. If you need to extend more excitement and drive, you can do such by expanded motioning. Over-motioning (mainly when hands are raised over the shoulders) can cause you to seem whimsical, less trustworthy, and less incredible.

- Laidback gestures—Arms held at midsection tallness, and motions inside that level plane, help you—and the group of spectators—feel focused and formed. Arms at the midsection and bowed to a 45-degree point (joined by a position about shoulder-width wide) will likewise assist you with keeping grounded, empowered, and centered.

In this quick-paced, techno-charged time of email, writings, video chats, and video visits, one generally accepted fact remain: Face-to-confront is the most liked, gainful, and impressive correspondence medium. The more business pioneers convey electronically, all the more squeezing turns into the requirement for individual communication.

Here's the reason:

In face to face gatherings, our brain processes the nonstop course of nonverbal signs that we use as the reason for building trust and expert closeness. Eye to eye collaboration is data-rich. We translate what individuals state to us just halfway from the words they use. We get a large portion of the message (and most passionate subtlety behind the words) from vocal tone, pacing, outward appearances, and other nonverbal signs. What's more, we depend on prompt input on others' quick reactions to assist us with checking how well our thoughts are being acknowledged.

Strong is the nonverbal connection between people. When we are in a certified affinity with somebody, we subliminally coordinate our body positions, developments, and even breathing rhythms with theirs. Most intriguing, in up close and personal experiences, the mind's "reflect neurons" impersonate practices, yet sensations and sentiments too. When we are denied these relational prompts and are compelled to depend on the printed or verbally expressed word alone, the cerebrum battles and genuine correspondence endures.

Innovation can be a great facilitator of factual data, but meeting in an individual is the key to positive relationships between employees and clients. Whatever industry you work in, we're always in the business of individuals. However, tech-savvy you could be, face-to-face gatherings are by far the most successful way of capturing attendees ' interest, engaging them in a discussion, and fostering fruitful teamwork. It is said that if it doesn't matter that much, send an email. If it is crucial for the task but not significant, make a phone call. If it is extremely important for the project's success, it is advised to see someone.

Chapter 6. How to Persuade People

Persuasion is a deliberate effort to change or alter a person's opinions, beliefs, or attitudes toward an issue, situation, object, or person. It is usually achieved by transmission of a message which could be verbal or symbolic.

While persuasion could be used in a manipulative sense, it is, in an actual purpose, different from manipulation. It is because, when persuading a person, he/she is usually aware of your efforts at changing their point of view and willingly or reluctantly allows you to try. In this instance, the person listens and concentrates on what you are saying and then tries to rationalize your ideas with reality before then putting whatever conclusions they come to comparison with what they believed.

Your role in the entire dynamic is to state your reasons for the change you are prescribing, give illustrations and evidence supporting your views and try to convince the target of your advances that your line of action or advice is their best bet. The main goal of this is getting them to switch to a state of reasoning. In this, persuasion resembles manipulation because your goal is still to push the target towards an outcome that they might ordinarily not have considered right.

The success attained in persuasion usually depends on the target's preconceptions and their strength, their perception of the person sharing the new message or idea, their perception of the message or idea, and finally, their perception of the conclusion on offer. Upon outlining these reasons, it should be clear to you that the subject of your effort would probably possess ideas that are at least dissimilar. If not contradictory to yours and as such, the entire process would either hinge on your persuasion being very convincing or the target's ability to meet a compromise between the conflicting ideas that would majorly mirror the changes you want.

Below are six major theories that explain how the human mind absorbs and reacts to information. Knowledge of these would greatly increase the odds of persuasion if you could pinpoint it in your target.

The Attribution Theory

It concludes that people would either attribute actions and characters to people and objects, respectively, either relative to the context they are being considered in or according to their emotional disposition.

When they attribute using context as a guide, they are likely to come to decisions that consider the environment of origin and situational factors. Such is seen when a person refrains from calling a product inferior or calling a person insensitive. Instead of arguing that the product has been made from the best possible items available to the manufacturer. The person is merely reacting as he has learned from his childhood environment.

However, when considering their emotional disposition, they tend to believe that whatever is convenient for them is the only right decision or approach for every other person. Consider this situation:

You meet a person at an event or gather and try to start a conversation with them, but instead of giving you a polite audience, the person appears preoccupied with their thoughts or acts aloof. Angered or annoyed, you walk away, and when asked for an opinion on the person, you characterize them as proud, arrogant, or self-important.

In this case, the characterization you have concluded is based solely on your emotional disposition and does not consider the situation or possible problems the other person might have. The idea is not to determine whether you are wrong or right but rather to analyze how you are likely to process information about people and things. You might be right about the person.

Another situation is when you have been accused of doing something wrong, and you claim that your accusers have failed to see things from your perspective and are only interested in their point of view.

It is a perfect example of considering things as regards context. In this case, probably because the things said are negative, you'd notice the emphasis placed on contextual understanding of actions. There is also a minor hint of the dispositional thinking coinciding.

The Conditioning Theory

In this case, the person is likely to do things. It is if they are conditioned to look like their own decisions instead of coercion. It is mostly utilized in the advertising industry where commercials, advertisements, and billboards convey information that would provoke positive feelings in the population of interest. They then connect such sentiments to their products, making you feel that the work would bring such a feeling into your life since you are more likely to purchase their product, thinking that your decision was an independent one.

It is usually possible because we generally perceive things based on our emotions and are more likely to buy things because they make us feel good.

The Cognitive Dissonance Theory

Based on this theory, it is assumed that people tend to aim for consistency in their thoughts, attitudes, and decisions. It is the cause why most individuals create principles that they strive to follow. Most people also seem intent on reconciling the contradictions as much as they can until they feel comfortable. I would give two examples of this.

Example 1

You have an extreme and deep-rooted need for canned food, either due to the laziness of having to cook meals or the frustrations at having to wait in queues for food. Then you are told that such canned meals could lead to cancer, and you don't want to have cancer. But you also don't want to stop eating canned food. So, instead of stopping with the habit, you comfort yourself that millions of people like you have the same habit and never have cancer.

The cancer theory might be untrue, but your eagerness to dispute the fact or at least make the consequences seem less severe is your own way of changing your mind or making the facts you have just learned seem less important or true. It is one of the ways of dealing with cognitive dissonance theory.

Example 2

Imagine a criminal with a conscience. It is probably hard to envision, but they do exist. Their criminal tendencies are clashing with their tender hearts and causing a bit of discomfort in such a situation. Such a person is very likely dealing with his/ her problems by giving in to the rationale that a criminal and wealthy life far outweighs the benefits of having a clean conscience or right heart.

Again, I am refraining from judging whether such a rationale is sound but am more focused on the fact that the person seems to give in to a motivation that overlaps with most people's general aim to deal with his discomfort.

The Judgment Theory

This one is straightforward to grasp. It merely proposes that when faced with a new piece of information or idea, a person's reaction is dependent on the way he/she currently feels on the topic. What this means is that we're likely to accept something that resonates with our current belief, reject something that doesn't fit in with our beliefs, or stay indifferent to something never considered before.

Therefore, when attempting to persuade a person, it is better first to determine their views on the topic to gauge whether you'd be successful and if your effort would eventually be worth it.

The Inoculation Theory

The inoculation theory supports the view that even if uninterested before in two points of view, once argued for, you are likely to pick the dominant point of view and stick with it. Here is an example:

You have never viewed a soccer game in your life, but one day you are relaxing on the beach and happen to find yourself stuck between two diehard soccer fans who support rival teams. An argument begins about whose team is better and more dominant, and they both turn to you, presenting their points like you are a seasoned fan and, after some time, ask you to judge who's better. You obviously would pick the person with the better argument to not betray your lack of knowledge on the subject. If another individual were to pose a question to you in the future, inquiring about which of those two teams is better, you'd probably find yourself arguing in favor of the choice you made then, maybe even with some of the same points that were used then.

It is the power of inoculations; the most powerful initial idea always takes root first.

Narrative Persuasion Theory

From experience, I think we would all accept that stories have a more enhanced effect on perception and opinions than abstract advice. People's attitudes and views towards objects and others tend to change when they are told compelling stories of such subjects.

The theory simply attempts to explain the heightened effect that can have on people if appropriately utilized. In this, the listener feels transported, which significantly affects their perception of events, making them more pronounced and vivid than they might have been if they had been expressed ordinarily and abstractly.

The Psychological Perspective

Ordinarily, persuading people would be difficult without the ability to organize and present an argument properly. But if inexperience in any or both of this is coupled with an inability to understand moods and stances. Your task would be made many times more likely to fail.

The ability to instantly sense and recognize a person's stance on an issue is difficult, not to talk of performing the same trick on an audience. Because of this difficulty, most speakers who are attempting to introduce people to a new point of view always tend to ask questions that would enable them to gauge the audience's stance before moving on with their presentation.

After asking such questions immediately, they usually watch out for visible reactions from the audience members, maybe a smile to indicate a knowledge of the topic, sitting up to indicate interest, turning away, or sighing to indicate disagreement, boredom, or even a person willing to answer. These simple markers give you an idea of how your message may be received and help you map out a strategy of approach. It is also a useful tool as people express themselves more sincerely when they do not feel particularly in the spotlight. If you are unsure, do not refrain from asking a few surface questions to test the waters or, more aptly, to feel out the crowd.

It should also be noted that numerous people might give an adverse reaction to one-on-one persuasion and would start arguments to further their points. The moment you realize that your attempt to persuade a person has deteriorated into an argument, it is sensible for you to stride away. Very few disputes occurring outside law courts ever get settled. Engaging in one would be fruitless and time-consuming. That time is better spent elsewhere.

Chapter 7. How to Analyze People

Logic alone cannot help you if you want to understand an individual. To know how to analyze the non-verbal initiative cues given off by people, you have to give in to the other vital forms of information. In order to do this, you have to give up any emotional baggage or preconceptions like ego clashes or old resentments that might be stopping you from clearly seeing someone—the clue to this to receive information neutrally without contorting it and staying objective.

Whether you are trying to read your kids, your partner, co-worker, or boss, in order to do so accurately, you have to bring down some walls and surrender to any biases. You have to willingly let go of old ideas that can be very limiting. Those who can analyze other people properly are trained to read and analyze the invisible. They have learned to look further than where people generally look by utilizing their "super senses" and can access life-changing intuitive insights.

Analyzing People Effectively

In order to recognize how your mannerisms and actions can affect other people, you have to be able to comprehend the alterations between how you communicate with different people and how you act around them.

You need to note how all these people's different behavior affects you and how your actions make you appear to them. A suitable method of practicing this is by thinking about how other people might behave around you based on how they consider you in their lives. Maybe they act in a different way around you than they do around other people.

People You Do Know vs. People You Don't

How you see and behave towards someone is greatly affected by how well you know them or how well you need to know them. Your closeness to someone or distance from someone in the aspect of your relationships will define the things you need to contemplate when you are analyzing both you're and the other person's behavior while you are interacting with them. In the end, this will also help you determine how you want to make use of these insights in order to analyze what they are trying to communicate with you correctly.

Here are four examples to better elaborate on this concept:

1. You have an unstable relationship with your mother. Your relationship is long-term and intensely involved. You aim to find out the origin of the complication and fix your relationship with her. To do this, you first need to consider a few things: how she fulfills her needs, her points of concentration, comprehensive information about her personal life, the way she communicates with you, her impulses, preferences, and her body language.

2. You are in a relationship with your significant other for about a year. As it's starting to get more serious, you consider asking him/her to move in with you. The relationship is intimate and medium-term. Your first objective should be to think whether moving in together would be a smart move. You want to figure out how they might respond when you ask them the question. The essential factors that you need to consider are their past experiences and personal life, how they communicate with

you, their impulses, preferences, and body language. Besides, you also need to consider how they go about fulfilling their requirements, their points of concentration, and their drive. You can also acquire more insight by consulting family and friends.

3. You are thinking about sharing innovation for a business idea with a co-worker. You have a relatively superficial relationship with this co-worker, and it is medium-term. You want to observe their behavior to determine whether the two of you are compatible to work together and whether he or she would be a suitable business partner before expressing your idea. You want to figure out how you should approach them to get the best response. You need to observe the following factors: how they verbally communicate with you, their impulses, preferences, and body language. In addition to that, defining their concentration and having some insight into their past experiences and personal life. It could also be beneficial in this case.

4. In the initial process of meeting someone, you might ask yourself whether they are attracted to you. You are attracted to them; however, before expressing your feelings to them, you want to get to know them better. At this time, your interpersonal relationship with this other person is superficial and relatively new. In addition to that, before expressing your feelings, you want to be sure that you are correctly interpreting their signals if the feelings are not mutual. You need to pay consideration to a few things with your first encounters with this person. Some of the influences you need to contemplate are their preferences, how they speak with you, their body language, and how they convey themselves around you. You can subtly acquire some details like their history with relationships in your first few conversations and use that information to determine how you will act.

Techniques by Which You Can Analyze People

- Sense emotional energy.

Our emotions well express the energy or "vibe" we give off. Our intuition helps us register these. Some people help improve our vitality and mood, and it feels good to be around them. However, others can be draining, and you just want to move away from them. Even though this subtle energy is invisible, it can be felt feet or inches from the body. It is known as chi in Chinese medicine. It's a vitality that is important to health.

Methods to Analyze Emotional Energy

1. Notice their laugh and tone of voice—A lot about our state of emotions can be conveyed via our voice's volume and tone. The frequencies of sounds create vibrations. Try to notice how the tone of someone's voice affects you while you are trying to analyze them. Ask yourself whether their style feels whiny, snippy, abrasive, or soothing.

2. Notice the feel of their touch, hug, and handshake—much like an electric current, emotional energy is also shared through physical contact. Ask yourself whether a hug or a handshake feels confident, comfortable, warm, or off-putting. Is the other person's hand limp, indicating that they are timid and non-committal? Or are they clammy, meaning anxiety?

3. Notice people's eyes—People's eyes send powerful energy. Studies have revealed that similar to the brain that sends electromagnetic signals beyond the body, and the eyes do this. Take time and try to watch people's eyes. Are they angry? Mean? Tranquil? Sexy? Caring? Also, try to understand whether someone seems to be hiding or guarding something or are at home in their eyes, revealing their capacity for intimacy.

4. Since their presence, someone's company is like an emotional atmosphere surrounding us like the sun or a rain cloud. It's not essentially congruent with behavior or words but is the overall energy emitted by us. While you are trying to analyze people, try to notice: Are you feeling scared, making you want to back off? Or are you attracted by their social presence?

Listen to Your Intuition

Intuition is not what your head says. It's what your gut feels. It is the non-verbal information you can perceive beyond logic, words, and body language. What counts the most when you want to understand someone is who they are from within and not just their outer appearance. With the help of intuition, you can reveal a richer story by seeing further than the obvious.

Some intuitive cues you can look into:

1. Look out for intuitive empathy—You can experience an intense form of empathy when you can feel people's emotions and symptoms in your body. Therefore, when you analyze people, try to notice whether you are upset or depressed after an uneventful meeting or if your back hurts suddenly. Get some feedback to determine whether this is empathy or not.

2. Watch out for flashes of insight—You might get an "ah-ha" about people while you are conversing about them. It might come in a flash, so stay alert. If not, you might miss out on it. These critical insights might get lost as we tend to move onto the next thought very fast.

3. Feel the goosebumps—Goosebumps are amazing intuitive signals that tell us when we resonate with people who say something that we connect with or when they inspire or move us. It can also take place when you feel a sense of déjà-vu. Déjà-

vu is a feeling of recognition that you might have known someone before, although you haven't met.

4. Honor your gut feelings—During your first meetings, try to listen to your gut. Before you even have an opportunity to ponder about it, a visceral reaction already takes place. It conveys whether you are relaxed or not. Gut feelings take place very fast as a primal response. They act as your internal truth meter and convey to you whether you can trust someone or not.

Observe Body Language Cues

According to studies, words account for only seven percent of our method of communication. The remaining is represented by our voice (thirty percent) and body language (fifty-five percent). Stay fluid and relaxed while reading body language cues. Don't get overly analytical or intense. Simple sit back, be comfortable, and observe.

1. Interpret facial expression—Our feelings and emotions tend to get stamped on our faces. The deep frown lines convey Overthinking or worry. The smile lines of joy are depicted by the crow's feet. Pursed lips signal bitterness, contempt, or anger. Grinding teeth or clenched jaw are signs of tension.

2. Pay attention to posture—When you are trying to analyze someone's posture, ask yourself: Is their chest puffed out when they are walking, which is a sign of a big ego? Or do they cower while walking, which is a sign of low self-esteem? Or, is their head held high, confident?

3. Notice their appearance—When you are analyzing others, pay attention to their appearance. Are they wearing a t-shirt and jeans, indicating that they are dressed casually for comfort? A

power suit with properly shined shoes that are indicating ambition and being dressed for success? Or a pendant like a Buddha or a cross displaying their spiritual values? Even a well-fitted top with cleavage, representing a seductive choice?

Learning how to analyze other people accurately takes time and practice, and obviously, every rule has some exceptions. However, you can improve your abilities to analyze others, communicate properly with them, and understand their thinking by keeping these points in mind while building your powers of observation.

Chapter 8. Dark Psychology Secrets

There is a concept in the world of psychology, which is called the dark triad. The obscure triad is a set of three personality traits, namely, Machiavellianism, narcissism, and psychopathy. This group of three is labeled dark, owing to the usual malignant habits correlated with certain characteristics. The dark triad's dramatic opposite is the lighter triad, which is a topic and debate for another book in itself. Although the three traits depicted on the dark triad in their studies are distinct, it is seen that they also overlap. It indicates that with blurred boundaries, a person who increases the success on the dark triad exam will likely have all these traits present. It might be hard to tell, for example, where narcissism stops and where psychopathy begins.

Discussions about the Dark Triad concept were initially begun in 1998. Three psychology experts do it. They asserted that Machiavellianism, narcissism, and psychopathology occurred overlappingly in normal samples. Two psychologists by the titles of Williams and Paulus would later invent a name for this group, in 2002: the dark triad.

There have often been discussions and debates about nature's part in seeking to comprehend the dark triad's personality traits. To put it simply, psychologists, behavioral scientists, and researchers were keen to know whether born or bred are Dark Triad persons. Are we born stupid and manipulative, or have we become so as a consequence of the things that we grow up to be exposed to? According to various research done, it has been noted that a dark triad has an important genetic basis to it. That is, some born with such susceptibility to the dark traits of the triad. However, in terms of heritability, narcissism, or psychopathy, rank greater than Machiavellianism. That is when contrasted to a parent that ranks high on the Machiavellian scale, a psychopathic mother or father is more willing to switch the characteristic to their offspring.

The dark triadic characteristics have also been seen to be underrepresented in top-level management in reports that might not be really friendly to someone working. When the dark triad elements are unpackaged in the segments below, it becomes evident why this recognition may be so.

Dark Triad: Narcissism

A narrative is revealed in the Greek myths of a young man named Narcissus. Narcissus was indeed a hunter renowned for his striking, good looks. Narcissus did not have a time of day for them, given the adoration he got from his admirers and even forced others to take their own lives to show their devotion. While there are several varieties of Narcissus's story, all of them refer to him being extremely self-absorbed, which eventually ended up in him going to die mortality that was retribution for his selfish ways. Thanks to the story of that young man, Sigmund Freud first coined the term narcissism. Freud, aptly titled On Narcissism in his famous 1914 essay.

In the simplest terms, narcissism is the increased and compulsive self-admiration which a person has towards himself and his personal features. A narcissist is always easy to recognize since they quickly offer away their behavior and values.

Asking yourself if you have a narcissist in their life? Here is what you should look for:

- Narcissists tend to feel good and always have the ability to be entitled.

- Type-A perfectionists are also narcissists.

- Narcissists have an unflagging thirst for control.

- Narcissists don't have a sense of limits.

How Do Narcissists Control People?

Now that you realize how well a narcissist looks, you're possibly curious about what the narcissist is doing to manipulate you in your life. How difficult can it be to remember, after all, that someone is attempting to manipulate you? The response is, it can be quite challenging, particularly when this person conceals their acts as only searching for you. Many narcissists are typically very clever and can fit in their daily life without drawing attention to them. They could also be very creative and talented, and the allure that tries to draw you to them will usually be that. When you're out there going to look for a narcissist-shaped monster, you might not be going to look for that skilled and super artistic friend who's always having a solution to everything. And still, she might be the only narcissist in the life who just thinks about competing or who gets injured along the way.

Narcissists are also quite keen liars, in addition to using their mentioned characteristics to the best of ability. Narcissists conduct routine the skill of deception in its various forms in a bid to be the celebrity of every show. Deception is the way the narcissist throws you off reality, so they stay in control. In either scenario, they always exist in an altered world where they are good, and everyone else is inferior to them. Hence, deceit is just a means for them to draw you through this repetitive story where they are the principal character.

Dark Triad: Machiavellianism

Niccolò Machiavelli, sometimes referred to as the founder of modern social science, was a Renaissance-era Italian who favored loads of hats. Machiavelli has been amongst others a historian, politician, poet, humanist, author, and diplomat. Machiavelli composed his most popular work, The Prince, in 1513. In this book, Machiavelli defined and advocated the usage of unscrupulous methods for obtaining and retaining political influence. The word Machiavellianism arose from this work and its endorsements, that was used to refer to the kind of politicians and tactics Machiavelli mentioned in his book. This word was later coined by psychology researchers to define a psychological characteristic marked by a lack of sympathy and a drive to succeed at the detriment of others, be it by deception, coercion, or the flouting of traditional dignity laws and morality. A person who displays Machiavellianism is, in the simplest form, willing to do almost anything if it meant playing. Machiavelli is the purpose of why the ending phrase justifies the means that exist.

Most work has been conducted since the introduction of the word Machiavellianism in philosophy to ascertain what determines the people who score highest on a Machiavellianism test, better known as high Mach's. High Mach's have been found to tend to value power, money, and competition above all else. High Mach's put a very cheap cost on things like building a community, family, and even love. Among those that score low above the Machiavellianism index, better known as low Mach's, the opposite is accurate.

Dark Triad: Psychopathy

Psychopathy is a feature of temperament marked mainly by a loss of empathy toward others. Psychopaths barely experience empathy for others and will rarely feel remorse even when other people have been hurt. There are various psychopathy views, but many of them always seem to agree on the three primary features that differentiate a psychopath from any normal individual. These three traits include fearlessness, lack of restraint, and meanness that any other person would consider uncomfortable.

Psychopaths are brave and aggressive and are not reluctant to step into new terrain even though they could be in danger. Although most individuals are usually overwhelmed by these conditions, psychopaths should be coping with such scenarios as if doing their everyday activities. Psychopaths often have a high degree of self-confidence as well as social boldness that allows them to interact with individuals without the shyness or anxiousness that others may have. Often, whenever a gruesome crime has been committed, you could perhaps hear about the nature of the investigation and shudder while going to think to yourself: how can a man live with himself for doing so? It's business as usual for a psychopath to kill someone and then grab a sunny face up at their local restaurant. It is not to say that all psychos have killed somebody. Some psychopaths instead rendered their lack of sympathy and susceptibility to other transgression and crimes.

Psychopaths show impaired regulation of the instinct, so they cannot regulate their impulses. When a regular human gets a desire of any kind, they can sometimes bring it under control and speak out of that state themselves. For instance, if you're having to deal with an irritating colleague who just won't be shutting up regarding their forthcoming bridal shower, you'll probably be able to combat the desire to slap them in their face. On the other hand, a psychopath will often be resolve by instinct and will react without giving it a second thought about the cost of everyone's decision. Psychopaths are susceptible to snapping in a simple way. Even one gets injured as they pop.

Common decency, when dealing with others, demands a certain level of decorum and kindness. It is not something of concern to psychopaths. While the majority of the people are worried about kindness and caring, the nicest person in the room will have no issue being a psychopath. Based on the situation in hand, they might be dramatic or execute about it.

The Dark Triad Practice

The dark triad test gauge how one score, as for the three practices of narcissism, Machiavellianism, or psychopathy, is concerned. The test is sometimes used in various settings, and by law courts and police in particular. The dark triad test is also used by corporations to gauge their employees. The primary reason the dark triad method is implemented is to assess an entity's personality characteristics and likely forecast their actions to prevent unsavory behaviors. It was noted that people who score high on the dark triad study are more likely to cause problems and social distress, whether in the work environment or even in their employment state. At the same time, these people will also likely have an easy time to attain leadership positions and gain sexual partners.

The dark triad test asks you to address a series of questions on a range of subjects like how you think about others and yourself, how you maintain track of details you could use to harm someone, and your general opinions on existence, death, and social experiences, among others. The dark triad test may be a nice way to gauge how you perform on the dark triad scale when self-administered. The dark triad test might not be very precise when administered by law courts and police as the respondent may purposely alter their answers to make them look better than it actually is. It is a primary drawback of the triad check in the night. If you're willing to take the dark triad exam, there are some online places where you'll be able to complete a study in minutes. Be careful to take the test results too personally—sometimes, the justifications you give are based on the kind of day you are taking and not on the type of person you are being. In any event, if you recognize yourself as a respectable human being who always respectfully treats others and never harms others, then you shouldn't worry very much about what an experiment says about you.

Chapter 9. How to Defend Ourselves of Dark Psychology

First, Identifying Them

By now, we have examined the foundations of dark psychology, the psychological profiles that make up the Dark Triad, typical forms of manipulation in relationships, and how manipulation has manifested itself in society's institutions.

First, remember that simply because you are not currently in a personal or professional relationship that could be defined as manipulative does not mean that you are free of all danger and concern. Predators have had to learn the hard way to live and achieve success using cold and calculating psychology from which they truly do not ever get any rest.

Imagine being injured in a serious accident and losing the use of one or more of your limbs. Regardless of how much you would prefer to have the use of that limb back. You will be forced to find some way to adapt. Emotional predators do the same thing. But because their injuries are invisible, and because of the business world's competitive nature, they sometimes hold an advantage over us if we fail to maintain vigilance.

Emotional predators can blend into the normal landscape because it is easy for them to go through daily living motions. They truly do not care if things don't work out because they have no value for their relationships or the things that society has established as having value.

Consider that the serial killer Ted Bundy worked on a crisis hotline while he stalked and murdered young women. He appeared successful, outgoing, handsome, and well-adjusted, but he was not. Or consider that the serial killer John Wayne Gacy, who murdered and buried in the crawl space beneath his home, almost 40 young men and boys, spent his days running a construction business, held fundraisers for local political leaders, and entertained sick children.

It may seem nauseating, especially with these extreme and dramatic examples. Still, for the emotional predator, society's important responsibilities are less a source of personal and professional satisfaction and fulfillment and more a perfect cover for their predatory addiction. As a result, you may find it helpful to develop some habits that will help you learn to classify some of the significant signs of emotionally predatory behavior.

Not everyone's life is perfectly organized or compartmentalized. Often environments and the people in them cross boundaries. Often in our daily lives, we wonder where things may have gone wrong. Quite often, the answer may be that we are trapped in a relationship with an emotional predator.

Regardless of the environment in which you meet people, you should always maintain a vigilant lookout for any of the following telltale signs of a predatory personality:

- Pathologically selfish people. They may go through friendship and love motions, but their emptiness is apparent when they fail to initiate social outings or when all encounters leave you feeling exhausted and drained.

- Emotional predators may offer lots of charm and flattery, but if there is a lack of substance to your interactions with them, you can be sure the compliments are probably false, too.

- Predators will exaggerate their accomplishments and even lie. If you call them on it, they will refuse to take responsibility or admit that they are wrong.

- A date or outing with an emotional predator may always be a high-stakes adventure. If you never seem able to engage with them simply over a cup of coffee and have a happy and fulfilling encounter, you may be dealing with a predator.

- Predators are bullies by nature and use anger as their primary means of communication. Avoid people who demonstrate a tendency to humiliate people or challenge anyone who seems to have more power or success than they do. Predators also use insults and putdowns to build themselves up. You may notice this kind of conduct directed at other people when you are out with a predator. For example, if you are at a café or restaurant, a predator may try to impress you by insulting or humiliating the staff.

- Predators are manipulative, which they often show by making promises and then not keeping them.

- Because predators lack a conscience and do not understand that their abusive behavior should make them feel bad, a telltale sign, maybe anyone who boasts about committing abusive actions or crimes

- Predators may also display parasitic behavior. If you are tangled with someone who is excessively lazy and uses you, you should find a way to end the relationship.

Guidelines

Of course, identifying the signs of predatory behavior is only half the battle. The other half is discovering a way to resolve the conflicts and repair the damage that inevitably follows in the wake of an encounter with an emotional predator.

The following are some general guidelines. Some of the tips are meant as suggestions that you should implement on a daily basis. They should become new habits that will now be part of your daily routine. It is important not to regard these tips as chores or burdensome or a diversion or interruption of your normal life. Think of these suggestions as your own personal investment in your daily professional development.

Suppose a virtuoso musician who plays violin for a symphony wants to stay at the top of his profession. In that case, no matter what else he does, one thing must remain constant: daily practice and a constant effort to stretch his repertoire by seeking out more challenging pieces, finding new forms of expression, and adding new skills to his resume. Consider a university professor in any department—being hired into a tenured position is the only beginning. The "publish or perish" mentality will soon take hold. He will find that continually refreshing his professional assessment of his area of expertise is as much a part of his daily professional routine as the more mundane tasks involved in classroom lectures.

So, it is with life in the modern world. To maintain a position of success and happiness and fulfillment, we must think like any gifted performer or professional. Constant vigilance and the continual addition of new weapons to your arsenal to fight the war against the growing threat of epidemic levels of emotional predation will keep your calendar full.

Buy a notebook, start a new spreadsheet, create a new folder in your favorite browser's bookmarks tab, and clear off a shelf on the bookcase in your office. This effort in your life can be just as much a passion and an investment in your success and happiness as the money you spent earning your college degree or the time and effort you spent building your professional network.

Most importantly, as we move down the list of tips for dealing with predators, remember that it is not unusual to find that recovery from such encounters, in some cases, may take years. Though the first step of dealing with a predator is ensuring, they are no longer physically present in your life. This step is not always easy to accomplish. And once you achieve this goal, actually repairing the damage they have caused may keep you very busy for some time to come. But relax—though the damage inflicted by emotional predators can grow increasingly worse over time, so the benefits of successfully dealing with these incursions can have increasingly beneficial returns over time.

Here are some suggestions:

Conduct A Self-Inventory

From time to time, read the details in the types of character traits that make people more susceptible to emotional predation. Look within and be truthful with yourself about your weaknesses. Don't do this as an exercise in self-abuse, though.

Consider that an emotional predator approaches you with only one goal in mind—to destroy you. You may not be entirely willing to examine yourself in an unflattering light, but an emotional predator who has made you a target may not have time for anything else.

Be Cautious

Whenever you are meeting new people, whether romantically or professionally, guard your personal information

Resist Projection and Gaslighting

When you encounter these environments, remind yourself that the goal is to defeat all genuine efforts to establish accountability.

Keep A Journal

You don't have to be eerie about it, but respect yourself enough to seriously take your personal and professional aspirations. Write down your thoughts and concerns at the end of the day, even if you can only manage a few sentences. The blank page will never pose the kind of threat to you that an emotional predator may.

By getting your complicated thoughts out of your head and on paper, you have unburdened yourself in a means that is most useful to you. A predator knows you have this need, and their willingness to listen may be designed as a trap.

Go "No Contact"

If you are in a professional or private relationship, and notice any of the signs of emotional predation, take steps immediately to end the relationship. Sometimes that may mean not replying to text messages, voice mail messages, or email messages. The predator may not like it and may react angrily, but if you try to enter into a negotiation or debate, you will be playing into their hands. Just say that you have decided not to respond any further, then stick to your plan.

Going "no contact," and in the modern world with all its digital communication, is a valid and acceptable tactic. If the predator continues to harass you, keep notes, and document their abuse. You may need to use it later if law enforcement becomes involved. Screenshots, text messages, email messages, and voice mail messages should all be saved and kept in a folder.

Get Help

Recognizing that you are in a relationship with a predator is the first step to escaping the relationship. Rescuing yourself must become your first priority. Remember that you will require professional help to solve this problem. If you are unsure how to proceed, take ten minutes out of your day, find a quiet place, and make a phone call. Don't worry about being perfect or feeling awkward. Professionals expect you to be at a loss and will know how to help.

Find A Support Network

You may need to seek the support of the law enforcement authorities. If you believe things are that bad, you are probably right. Don't let yourself be bullied or intimidated. As with a psychologist or helpline call, making the first call is the most important step. Even if things don't go exactly the way you think they should, by informing the local authorities, you will have placed yourself in a better position

Reinvent Yourself

Remember that as a victim of emotional predation, you will no longer be the person you once were and will have to restructure your thoughts and approaches to life.

Cheer Up

You have taken the first step toward defeating the predatory influences that have brought the dark cloud over your life. It is the first day of the rest of your life, not the last day of the life you used to live.

As you move forward with your new awareness of your surroundings' nature, the world may become a less intimidating place, and you will once again find the joy and happiness that seems to have been lost for so long.

Conclusion

The hands have a power that we do not know at all, and we ignore it. They send a huge number of messages that most people can't get.

Hands have always been used in conversation, and their meaning has changed countless times over the years. An example is a handshake.

The act of shaking hands finds its roots in the past. When the ancient tribes met, they used to show their palms to show that they were not hiding anything.

The Roman Empire instead used to tighten the forearm, so both people were sure that the other did not hide anything under his sleeve. It was done because, in those days, it was normal going around with a knife under the sleeve and being safe. They adopted this habit.

But like all the customs that have passed from generation to generation, the one used by the Romans has turned into our handshake.

This gesture for us is used in a myriad of different situations. They were ranging from the classic greeting with friends to a handshake to establish a working agreement between two large multinationals.

Even in Japan, where the classic greeting has always been the bow, the handshake is widely used today.

The fact that it is now a widespread gesture does not mean that it is simple to do. Behind the handshake, there is a real-world of domination and submission.

Still, in ancient Rome, two people greeted each other with an arm-wrestling handshake, I define it.

In other words, it was not common to shake hands as we do today, but one person took the hand of the other from bottom to top and created the shape of a sandwich, so to speak. The most powerful person dominated the other.

Nowadays, this practice is not used, but the person you win always exists while handshaking. There are three different types of endings for a handshake, which are:

- Dominance

- Submission

- Equality

These attitudes are perceived at the unconscious level, and our body processes them in a particular way, and each of these can decide in which direction the conversation will go.

An example I can give you is that of a study done on some company managers.

Male or female makes no difference.

It has shown that 89% of them use the dominant handshake and always hold out their hand first so that they can control the handshake accurately.

The exact opposite is a submissive handshake. In this case, the person puts his hand palm up, granting the other person dominance. A bit like dogs do when they lie down and put their bellies to the sky.

You can use this handshake if you want your interlocutor to feel in control of the situation. You can use this squeeze when you go to make excuses, for example.

On the other hand, when the two people are in a position in which both want to turn the other's hand to dominate, a "bite" is created. It causes the people to be equal, and neither of them, in the end, gets the better.

So, if you want to create an equal relationship with the person in front of you, avoid him turning your hand, but most importantly, use the same amount of force that he uses.

Now let's use hypothetical numbers. If he applies a force of 9 out of 10 to the handshake and you apply one of 7 out of 10, you will have to increase the strength, or you will be dominated. The same thing you will have to do in reverse if you don't want to dominate.

In short, if he applies a force of 5 and you of 7, if you do not want to be seen dominant, you will have to lower the power of your grip forcefully.

But now I'll tell you a trick to never let yourself be dominated. Not even if you were to meet the president of the united states.

Indeed, with this technique, you will always and I repeat, always dominate the other. Always if in that situation you want to do it.

The technique is called "disarming the doers."

The technique consists of putting the arm outstretched with the palm facing down to not leave any escape for your interlocutor, and he will have to turn his hand and put himself in submission forcefully.

From that moment on, you can do whatever you want. You decide whether to dominate or be equal, but it will be very difficult for him to bring the situation in his favor.

A bit like it happens in games when you are three points above your antagonist, and the game is about to finish, he has to do a miracle to win; indeed, the options for him are to draw or to lose.

If you occur to find yourself in the situation where a person holds out his hand as described above, there is something you can do to reverse the situation.

Step forward with your left foot and make sure to bring his hand vertically. This practice is not simple because we tend to advance with the right, but you will see that it will come more than natural to you with a little training.

If you really can't take this step, there is another way to save yourself from domination, and that is the double catch.

When the other brings you to palm up, you use the other hand, free to return the hold to a tie. So right now, you are using two hands while he is using just one.

Staying on The Left Is an Unfair Advantage

During a handshake, your position is crucial, and staying on the left helps a lot if you want to dominate.

It happens because, on the right, you have no control over the situation, while on the left, you can actually do it.

Kennedy liked this technique very much, even if at that time, nothing was known about body language; he already applied it by intuition.

If you go to see all the photos where he meets with leaders and famous people, you will always find him on the left with the double grip.

A striking example of how Kennedy was a phenomenon with body language is when he won the Nixon election.

At that time, it was renowned that the people who only heard the two politicians' speeches were convinced that Nixon had won while those who watched the scene agreed otherwise.

It led Kennedy to win the election. Pretty important this body language, isn't it?

However, going back to the speech above, if you are on the right of the photo to be able to have an equal situation, reach out to force him to shake your hand as you want.

To conclude, I give you a summary.

Few people know what an impression they can make on a stranger, even if they are conscious of how vital it is to yield a great starting point in a conversation.

Take some time to experiment with the various handshakes with perhaps friends, relatives, or work colleagues to get familiar with it. During important moments you will know how to behave correctly.

www.ingramcontent.com/pod-product-compliance
Lightning Source LLC
Chambersburg PA
CBHW071120030426
42336CB00013BA/2151